Hope Beyond Tears

Johnnie Mae McCall

Hope Beyond Tears

Johnnie Mae McCall

All rights reserved. No part of this publications may be reproduced, distributed, or transmitted in any form or by any means, including photocopying, recording, or other electronic or mechanical methods, without the prior written permission of the publisher, except in the case of brief quotations embodied in critical reviews and certain other noncommercial uses permitted by copyright law.

Unless otherwise notes, all scriptures are taken from The King James Version.

Published by "J. Mae McCall & Co."

Printed in the United States of America

**U.S. Copyright © 2021 No. 1-10470359231
ISBN: 978-1-7369517-0-5**

~Dedication~

In memory of the Late Richard Cobb

You showed us that trials will turn into triumph if we only endure until the end. You taught us that in life, we must persevere until our change comes. Today, it is through your legacy that we now stand firm, having hope that our darkest night will birth tomorrow's dawn, and tears of sorrow will become tears of joy.

~Thank You~

I would like to say thank you first to the creator of all things who breathe the wind of potential into my very existence. With that breath, I now exhale what has been placed in my womb from the beginning of my existence.

To Apostle Cierra Jones, I thank God for your covering, prayers, and leadership. You are God's gift to my life, and your leadership is God-driven. Thank you for continually pushing me to move beyond. I can honestly say that I have matured and tap into a new frequency that has propelled me into maturity. You have graced my life and walked me through many deliverance levels, and I am thankful for this. Apostle Kirby Gant, I honor you, Prophetess Annie Jones; you have graced my life and instilled that "It is possible."

Bishop George Searight, while sitting in the congregation one Sunday morning prayerfully in 2012, I watched by way of the spirit. I caught what was released by the spirit as you minister to one of the sisters grieving due to the loss of a loved one.

Pastor Mary Searight, you demonstrated love as the young woman sat crying and was ushered out of the congregation. From that moment nearly 8 years ago, this word was locked up and waiting to be released. Yes, Hope Beyond Tears.

Pastor Roderick Allen and Elder Sheila D. Allen, it is with a heart of love I acknowledge you, for it was you who showed me strength in my weakest hour. You showed me how to minister through and with grief. Today I am made the better, for there is grace for all of our grief.

Prophet Cliff Daniels and Lady Dionne Daniels, you will never know the strength and wisdom I have gained; and the momentum I have picked up by the spirit by sitting at your feet. Pastor Sheryl Price and Aligned for His Glory Ministry I am proud to be a part of the intercessors you lead. Pastor David and Ruth Budericki, thank you for the Elijah Inner Healing Classes. You will never know how much these classes helped me with inner healing for this project.

Dr. James P. Williams (Dean) and the United Bible School Facility thank you for nurturing my gift.

Elder Ingga Brockington and Elder Rhonda Scott of Handmaiden Prayer Ministries have prayed me through on many occasions.

My prayer partner Sister Michele Madison, Patricia Pair, thank you for being consistent in prayer with me. To Pansy, Sarah, Janet, and Anthony, and my big sister Dorothy Daniels I love you for allowing me to operate as the Evangelist in your life. To my aunt's Wanda, Chalmane, I had you in mind as I pushed forward in this project. Thank you for believing in the manifestation of good works. To my mothers, you know who you are, Aunt Betty. Mom Madison, Mother Dale, Ma Vicky, Mother Toye, Mom McMurray, and the others, I love you.

Finally, to all of you who thought it not robbery and decided to purchase a copy of this book, may you be blessed to know that no matter what the current winds of adversity blow, our God is the master over every form of grief, and he will cause the winds to cease in due time.

Weeping may endure for a night, but joy comes in the morning. Psalms 30:5

Table of Contents

Foreword 8

Introduction 9

Chapter 1: How Did We Get Here? 15

Chapter 2: I Can't Believe This Is Happening To Me .. 27

Chapter 3: Darkness Appears 47

Chapter 4: Where Is Hope 67

Chapter 5: Cup of Tears 85

    Things to Remember 107

Chapter 6: The Shadow of Hopes 109

Chapter 7: Hope Beyond The Tears 117

Conclusion 130

Prayer of Comfort 133

    Things to Remember 136

Resources and References 138

Bibliography 142

~Foreward~

Grace and Peace be unto you,

I know God has anointed and appointed the Author to share and bring hope to those who have experienced a loss. The journey she has traveled has allowed her to experience times of tears. Still, God being omnipotent and gracious in His infinite mercy has a purpose in our calamity to unveil His glory and strength. God ordained His glory and power to be revealed through Johnnie's experiences, and she will share with you His grace and eternal love that heals and gives unexplainable strength to go on and declare Him in the earth.

Hold on, for God has sent someone, in the name of Johnnie Mae McCall, to lift your spirit and speak life so you can see the purpose of God and live. This book will allow the tears of pain and sorrow to cease and dissipate, for God will dry all the tears from your eyes. He is touched by the feelings of our infirmities. As the griever releases the tears and embraces God's transforming power, they will see God's unchanging love, and soon the griever will label this time as a pivotal time that they have Embraced the Father.

Submitted by Elder Elect Lady Sheila D.
Allen True Vine Life Center

~Introduction~

Hope is the emotional state that promotes a positive outcome related to events and circumstances in one's life. Hope is the "feeling that what is wanted can be had or that events will turn out for the best." It is the act of looking forward to something with desire and reasonable confidence.

In the world we live in today, many have lost hope because of different forms of grief. Grief can be described as mental anguish, as that arising from bereavement. It is the normal process of reacting to a loss. The loss may be physical (such as death), social (such as divorce), or occupational (such as a job). Emotional reactions of grief can include anger, guilt, anxiety, sadness, and despair. Physical reactions of grief can include sleeping problems, changes in appetite, physical problems, or illness. Whatever form it functions, we must understand that there is good grief and bad grief. Good grief can be defined as a grieving experience turned into a positive, creative experience. Bad grief would be considered major depression with feelings of no recovery. John 10:10 states "that the thief comes to rob, kill and destroy but eternal life is a guaranteed promise if we would connect with our creator."

To have no hope is to live without expectancy for your tomorrow. This would be considered as a blind spot delivered by the enemy to stagnate you from movement. The job of the master deceiver is to cripple you with the spirit of oppression that will lead you to depression.

To have a clear understanding, let us define the word Oppression. Oppression is defined as an unjust or cruel exercise of authority or power. It is a sense of being weighed down in body or mind. There are five faces to oppression, and they are listed below:

1. Powerlessness – Lacks the power to get up

2. Helpless –Unable to defend oneself

3. Doom - Condemnation

4. Gloomy – Partially or totally dark

5. Loves Isolation – Has an affection for isolation

Each of the five forms of oppression overlaps with the other. Each is related to and reinforced by the many ideological-isms and phobias that exist in our society. The five ways of looking at oppression help us see that people cannot be divided neatly into the "oppressed and the oppressor." The master of deception always stands behind the scenes, waiting to dress the griever in another garment called depression.

Depression may be described as feeling sad, blue, unhappy, miserable, or down in the dumps. True clinical depression is a mood disorder in which feelings of sadness, loss, anger, or frustration interfere with everyday life for weeks or longer. Depression can change or distort the way you see yourself, your life, and those around you. People who have depression usually see everything with a more negative attitude. They cannot imagine that any problem or situation can be solved positively. I must make a declaration today that as you walk through your process of any form of grief, there is hope on the other side of your tears.

Jeremiah 29:11 is a clear indicator that we have a future with an expected end with the proper vision. While walking through the process of grief, many that view from the outside will suggest that you get over it quickly, but I must say walk through it and learn the lessons that will be given to you. As you walk through your process, you will realize that you have been given grace for your grief, and you are never alone Hebrews 13:5. As you walk through your grief, you will acknowledge that your process is a journey.

Chapter 1
How Did We Get Here

Whenever change takes place in our lives, we must ask ourselves questions. Proverbs 4: 7 states getting wisdom is the wisest thing you can do! And whatever else you do, develop good judgment. The writer simply said that wisdom prescribes the best end and the means best calculated for its attainment.

Understanding directs to the ways, times, places, and opportunities of practicing the lessons of wisdom. Wisdom points out the thing requisite; understanding sees to the accomplishment and attainment. Wisdom sees but understanding feels. One discovers, and the other possesses.

With understanding, we will understand how the human race entered on the platform of grief.

The fall of mankind opened the entire human race into a catastrophe. The word catastrophe is an event causing significant and often sudden damage or suffering; it is the denouement of a drama.

Other words that define the word catastrophe are disaster, calamity, or accident. If one must note, each word leads to the pathway of destruction. It is a complete failure.

Indeed, man lost his first estate and was ushered into death. It was in this particular moment we find mankind spiraling into a downward posture.

Mankind had an abundance of all things. Nothing was missing, nothing lacking, and finally, nothing broken. After all, He was in the image of He that created all things. Death or grief was not a part of mankind's vocabulary, nor was it released into the atmosphere.

The only words the trees of the earth, the fish of the sea; the beast of the field and mankind heard echo in the earth were from God's mouth. The word that was continually resounding was" It was good."

Today, we must do a sound check to hear what words are resounding in our ears? Are they words that will produce life, or are they words that will literally paralyze you from reaching your fullest potential?

Continuing forward, we see that all mankind had to do was live according to the laws and principles and daily walk in His dominion power. When man failed to obey his connection with God, he slipped into another posture. Losing His place postured him to be uncovered and stood him at death's doorway of grief and gloom.

Grief and gloom are two of the most miserable spirits on this earth. Once you welcome them in, they will want to make their abode within the person and usher the individual into a deeper place of darkness.

It is here we must allow Adam and Eve to testify Genesis 2:15 -25, and the chapter deals with the struggle. Come let us review the text with the author.

Genesis 2:15-25

New International Version (NIV)

15 The LORD God took the man and put him in the Garden of Eden to work it and take care of it.

16 And the LORD God commanded the man, "You are free to eat from any tree in the garden;

17 but you must not eat from the tree of the knowledge of good and evil, for when you eat from it you will certainly die."

18 The LORD God said, "It is not good for the man to be alone. I will make a helper suitable for him."

19 Now the LORD God had formed out of the ground all the wild animals and all the birds in the sky. He brought them to the man to see what he would name them; and whatever the man called each living creature, that was its name.

20 So the man gave names to all the livestock, the birds in the sky and all the wild animals. But for Adam no suitable helper was found.

21 So the LORD God caused the man to fall into a deep sleep; and while he was sleeping, he took one of the man's ribs and then closed up the place with flesh.

22 Then the LORD God made a woman from the rib he had taken out of the man, and he brought her to the man.

23 The man said, "This is now bone of my bones and flesh of my flesh; she shall be called 'woman,' for she was taken out of man."

24 That is why a man leaves his father and mother and is united to his wife, and they become one flesh.

25 Adam and his wife were both naked, and they felt no shame.

Genesis 3

New International Version (NIV)

The Fall

3 Now the serpent was more crafty than any of the wild animals the LORD God had made. He said to the woman, "Did God really say, 'You must not eat from any tree in the garden'?"

2 The woman said to the serpent, "We may eat fruit from the trees in the garden,

3 but God did say, 'You must not eat fruit from the tree that is in the middle of the garden, and you must not touch it, or you will die.'"

4 "You will not certainly die," the serpent said to the woman.

5 "For God knows that when you eat from it your eyes will be opened, and you will be like God, knowing good and evil."

6 When the woman saw that the fruit of the tree was good for food and pleasing to the eye, and also desirable for gaining wisdom, she took some and ate it. She also gave some to her husband, who was with her, and he ate it.

7 Then the eyes of both of them were opened, and they realized they were naked; so they sewed fig leaves together and made coverings for themselves.

8 Then the man and his wife heard the sound of the LORD God as he was walking in the garden in the cool of the day, and they hid from the LORD God among the trees of the garden.

9 But the LORD God called to the man, "Where are you?"

10 He answered, "I heard you in the garden, and I was afraid because I was naked; so I hid."

11 And he said, "Who told you that you were naked? Have you eaten from the tree that I commanded you not to eat from? "

12 The man said, "The woman you put here with me —she gave me some fruit from the tree, and I ate it."

13 Then the LORD God said to the woman, "What is this you have done?"

The woman said, "The serpent deceived me, and I ate."

14 So the LORD God said to the serpent, "Because you have done this, "Cursed are you above all livestock and all wild animals! You will crawl on your belly and you will eat dust all the days of your life.

15 And I will put enmity between you and the woman, and between your offspring and hers; he will crush your head, and you will strike his heel."

16 To the woman he said, "I will make your pains in childbearing very severe; with painful labor you will give birth to children. Your desire will be for your husband, and he will rule over you."

17 To Adam he said, "Because you listened to your wife and ate fruit from the tree about which I commanded you, 'You must not eat from it,'

"Cursed is the ground because of you; through painful toil you will eat food from it all the days of your life.

18 It will produce thorns and thistles for you, and you will eat the plants of the field.

19 By the sweat of your brow you will eat your food until you return to the ground, since from it you were taken; for dust you are and to dust you will return."

20 Adam[c] named his wife Eve,[d] because she would become the mother of all the living.

21 The LORD God made garments of skin for Adam and his wife and clothed them.

22 And the LORD God said, "The man has now become like one of us, knowing good and evil. He must not be allowed to reach out his hand and take also from the tree of life and eat, and live forever."

23 So the LORD God banished him from the Garden of Eden to work the ground from which he had been taken.

24 After he drove the man out, he placed on the east side of the Garden of Eden cherubim and a

flaming sword flashing back and forth to guard the way to the tree of life.

Born of the first estate, we see the man and the woman having everything pertaining to life. With this fall, one must note the garment of grief in every form of it; from the highest to the lowest degree was placed upon our human race.

Because of this statement, the testimony of Job and David should be announced. Job declared in chapter 14 and the 1st verse a man born of a woman is of a few days and full of trouble. He was literally declaring how frail humanity is, how short is life, which gives so much stress. Here, it entreats God for favor by the shortness of his life and certainty of death. He understood by sin, the creature is subject to corruption.

The word corruption in the Merriam-Webster dictionary is defined as impairment of integrity, virtue, or moral principle. In short terminology, it simply means that man began to decay. The word decay is to rot, lose strength or deteriorate. An excellent example of decay is when fruit begins to rot. Theologians would consider the term depravity. In the authors' dictionary, she would declare man was no longer pure or correct.

As David came on the scene, he testified powerfully he had to walk through the valley of the shadow of death. But if truth be told, he would fear no evil; for he understood that God was with him; and His rod and staff would comfort Him. (ASV)

Now that you understand how death came about, let us continue on to the meat of the matter. Today, if you are reading this book, you or someone close to you has been touched by hopelessness and grief. If you have not kept on living and you too will be affected.

Chapter 2
I Can't Believe This Is Happening To Me

This chapter deals with the initial news of your tragedy or calls to grief. It could be the loss of a dear family member, or the devastating blow of your husband abandoning you, or the loss of a job after 25 years, or losing a longtime friend. Nevertheless, we were never meant to experience the pain of losing.

Allow the author to share some initial shocking news with you that propelled her into the process of grief. It was nearly ten years ago I could remember receiving the shocking news of my brother's tragedy. It was a busy day at work when I received the call of his fate. After receiving the news in shock, I immediately stopped everything I was doing and headed down to the hospital.

Upon arrival, I found my brother lying in the hospital bed; he had been beaten and robbed. This news was a real shocker to me. Tell me, please, someone; how could this be; one day, you are healthy, and two days later, you are placed on life support. To the reader, five days later, he expired. I must declare unto you receiving the news through every phase of this event was a real shocker to my family and me.

Rehearsing the scene in my head, I could hear the words ringing out; he has expired, and all I could say to myself was, "this is not the way it was supposed to be." Is this really happening? Questions continually developing as I process the news; someone help me, please silence the noise.

Standing in shock, I continue to confess, "This is not happening to me." Indeed, it is happening, and I must silence the noise and stand back to regroup.

We find the griever has received the news, and reality really hasn't kicked in yet. So, the griever stands in a motionless posture at the moment, trying to process what they have just received.

The mind has the ability to accept or reject the news it has been given. To accept means in this moment of reality, I will deal with my current issue. To reject simply means you received the news but will process it at a later time. Processing at a later time simply allows you to set yourself up for oppression and depression.

Remember this, time is crucial, and you are opened to vulnerability. To be vulnerable means one is open to assault. This could be considered a weak moment for those that stand on the bridge of receiving news that will produce grief.

Let us allow a man and women from the Bible to show us their vulnerable stage when they received bad news, which produced grief. You see, grief does not necessarily mean someone died. Its entrance is smooth, but its effect could be horrific. Grief can take on many faces, and at any given moment, mankind could be dressed in its garment.

Take a journey with the author as she brings the grievers Adam and Eve to center stage once again. I know you just read these scriptures but now let us look at this word from the message bible: and how vulnerability set the stage for shocking news.

Genesis 2

The Message (MSG)

Heaven and Earth were finished, down to the last detail.

2-4 By the seventh day God had finished his work. On the seventh day he rested from all his work. God blessed the seventh day. He made it a Holy Day Because on that day he rested from his work, all the creating God had done.

This is the story of how it all started, of Heaven and Earth when they were created.

Adam and Eve

5-7 At the time GOD made Earth and Heaven, before any grasses or shrubs had sprouted from the ground—GOD hadn't yet sent rain on Earth, nor was there anyone around to work the ground (the whole Earth was watered by underground springs)—GOD formed Man out of dirt from the ground and blew into his nostrils the breath of life. The Man came alive—a living soul!

8-9 Then GOD planted a garden in Eden, in the east. He put the Man he had just made in it. GOD made all kinds of trees grow from the ground, trees beautiful to look at and good to eat. The Tree-of-Life was in the middle of the garden, also the Tree-of-Knowledge-of-Good-and-Evil.

10-14 A river flows out of Eden to water the garden and from there divides into four rivers. The first is named Pishon; it flows through Havilah where there is gold. The gold of this land is good. The land is also known for a sweet-scented resin and the onyx stone. The second river is named Gihon; it flows through the land of Cush. The third river is named Hiddekel and flows east of Assyria. The fourth river is the Euphrates.

15 GOD took the Man and set him down in the Garden of Eden to work the ground and keep it in order.

16-17 GOD commanded the Man, "You can eat from any tree in the garden, except from the Tree-of-Knowledge-of-Good-and-Evil. Don't eat from it. The moment you eat from that tree, you're dead."

18-20 GOD said, "It's not good for the Man to be alone; I'll make him a helper, a companion."

So GOD formed from the dirt of the ground all the animals of the field and all the birds of the air. He brought them to the Man to see what he would name them. Whatever the Man called each living creature, that was its name. The Man named the cattle, named the birds of the air, named the wild animals; but he didn't find a suitable companion.

21-22 GOD put the Man into a deep sleep. As he slept he removed one of his ribs and replaced it with flesh. GOD then used the rib that he had taken from the Man to make Woman and presented her to the Man.

23-25 The Man said, "Finally! Bone of my bone, flesh of my flesh!

Name her Woman for she was made from Man." Therefore, a man leaves his father and mother and embraces his wife. They become one flesh. The two of them, the Man, and his Wife, were naked, but they felt no shame.

Genesis 3

The Message (MSG)

1 The serpent was clever, more clever than any wild animal GOD had made. He spoke to the Woman: "Do I understand that God told you not to eat from any tree in the garden?"

2-3 The Woman said to the serpent, "Not at all. We can eat from the trees in the garden. It's only about the tree in the middle of the garden that God said, 'Don't eat from it; don't even touch it or you'll die.'"

4-5 The serpent told the Woman, "You won't die. God knows that the moment you eat from that tree, you'll see what's really going on. You'll be just like God, knowing everything, ranging all the way from good to evil."

6 When the Woman saw that the tree looked like good eating and realized what she would get out of it—she'd know everything!—she took and ate the fruit and then gave some to her husband, and he ate.

7 Immediately the two of them did "see what's really going on"—saw themselves naked! They

sewed fig leaves together as makeshift clothes for themselves.

8 When they heard the sound of GOD strolling in the garden in the evening breeze, the Man and his Wife hid in the trees of the garden, hid from GOD.

9 GOD called to the Man: "Where are you?" 10 He said, "I heard you in the garden and I was afraid because I was naked. And I hid."

11 GOD said, "Who told you, you were naked? Did you eat from that tree I told you not to eat from?"

12 The Man said, "The Woman you gave me as a companion, she gave me fruit from the tree, and, yes, I ate it." GOD said to the Woman, "What is this that you've done?"

13 "The serpent seduced me," she said, "and I ate."

14-15 GOD told the serpent: "Because you've done this, you're cursed, cursed beyond all cattle and wild animals, cursed to slink on your belly and eat dirt all your life. I'm declaring war between you and the Woman, between your offspring and hers. He'll wound your head; you will wound his heel."

16 He told the Woman: "I'll multiply your pains in childbirth; you'll give birth to your babies in pain. You'll want to please your husband, but he'll lord it over you."

17-19 He told the Man: "Because you listened to your wife and ate from the tree That I commanded you not to eat from, 'Don't eat from this tree,' The very ground is cursed because of you; getting food from the ground Will be as painful as having babies is for your wife; you'll be working in pain all your life long. The ground will sprout thorns and weeds, you'll get your food the hard way, Planting and tilling and harvesting, sweating in the fields from dawn to dusk, until you return to that ground yourself, dead and buried; you started out as dirt, you'll end up dirt."

20 The Man, known as Adam, named his wife Eve because she was the mother of all the living.

21 GOD made leather clothing for Adam and his wife and dressed them.

22 GOD said, "The Man has become like one of us, capable of knowing everything, ranging from good to evil. What if he now should reach out and take fruit from the Tree-of-Life and eat, and live forever? Never—this cannot happen!"

23-24 So GOD expelled them from the Garden of Eden and sent them to work the ground, the same dirt out of which they had been made. He threw them out of the garden and stationed angel-cherubim and a revolving sword of fire east of it, guarding the path to the Tree-of-Life.

The author sheds light on the two grievers' experiences in a vulnerable place because of the text. It is here we also view the garden experience. Nevertheless, grief authentically presents itself.

Adam and Eve the Garden Experience Another Form of Grief

In Genesis 2 and 3, we find the command given by God to Adam. In complete fellowship with God, we see a demonstration of perfection by both male and female. It is in chapter 3; we see the good news vs. bad news syndrome being displayed.

In Chapter 2, we see good news was being declared! Adam declared that the woman God gave him was bone of his bone and flesh of His flesh. In chapter 3, we see the terrible news he declared the woman he gave him did this thing. Could you imagine Eve's initial shock when she heard these words uttered out of the man's mouth? Something to think about, right! No doubt in her mind she was angry, upset, and filled with rage because of her grief. (Please note these are only some of the emotions expressed by anyone who grieves).

Just imagine this, the creator of the universe that gave them liberty now announces judgment because of the depravity of mankind. His words were gentle, but they also cut to the core as he declared unto the women:

Eve

1. I will make your pains in childbearing very serve; with painful labor, you will give birth to children.

2. Your desire will be for your husband, and he will rule over thee

Then he speaks to the man Adam, and he declares:

Adam

1. Because you listened to your wife and ate fruit from the tree about which I commanded you, you must not eat from it, cursed be the ground because of it all the days of your life. It will

produce thorns and thistles for you, and you will eat plants of the field.

2. By the sweat of your bow, you will eat your food. Since you were taken from the dust and back to the dust, you will return.

To the reader at this moment, just imagine the grief the first humans felt. Talking about initial news, this was enough to stop both Adam and Eve in their tracks, but because of God's grace, there appeared a shadow of hope. God gave them both a glimpse of hope when he decreed and declared the seed of the woman would bruise the serpent's head in *Genesis 3:15*. This enables both Adam and Eve to breathe in and catch their breath and move forward.

To the reader, when the initial news of any loss comes your way, it will always take on the faces listed below:

1. Unexpectedly vs. Expected State

In the typical posture, you expectedly have a knowing that loss will take place. For example:

(A terminally ill patient living in the last stage of the disease. Note, but when it happens, you still feel unexpectedly in total shock.

2. Suddenly

Abruptly, all at once (Example: Your son has been locked up for a traffic ticket, and you get a call from the hospital stating he is dead.)

3. Shockingly Highly disturbing emotionally

Highly offensive, indecent, or distasteful.

Very vivid or intense in tone

(Example: You receive a call with screaming and an announcement that your loved one is gone.)

No matter how you receive the news, it will be of initial shock because of the above faces. As human beings, we were designed to be free, having no limitations or boundaries. So, you see, when grief is announced, the shock is triggered only because of the curse.

In remembrance of the curse, mankind will always be shifted back to their first moment of grief, where they were dressed in the garden with it. The reader must be reminded that we were made to be eternal beings, never existing with any form of grief.

When receiving the initial news, remember the enemy will instantly employ his staff to take you up and out to reroute your course. It is crucial to stay present at the moment.

Breathe. It is easier said than done, but you must try to quiet the mind and body. When our bodies are under stress, the adrenal gland secretes the hormone cortisol. Higher levels of cortisol can put someone at greater risk for heart disease. We must try to calm ourselves, as hard as it might be. Sometimes closing your eyes for a few minutes and focusing on your breath can be helpful. Ask yourself positive questions to resolve your emotions, but the key is to stay focus. You must tell yourself this is not the end of the world.

There are lessons to be learned in every stage of your grief walk. So, remember, when you receive the news, lean on God's wisdom to get you through the initial news. Proverbs 3:6 declares we must acknowledge the Lord in all our ways, and He will direct our paths.

Oh, that we might know the Lord! Let us press on to know him. He will respond to us as surely as the arrival of dawn or the coming of rains in early springs declare *Hosea 6:3*

It is a must you take on the mind of Christ by eating the word of God and allowing yourself to be around intercessors who pray for you to combat the spirit of oppression and depression and remember this it's okay to cry.

A renewed mind will help you be adorned with beauty for ashes, and the joy of the Lord will become your inner strength. In most of this book, I will share many of my life lessons of grief and loss. That will become tools for turning your sadness into joy.

As you get over the initial shock, you will be able to declare Oh yes, this is happening to me, Now Lord, what lesson will you allow me to learn as I face my next moments' grief. Please hold my hand and walk me through this process. This is too much for me to bear. True confession births total healing.

Psalms 23:1-2

The Lord is my Shepherd; I shall lack nothing. He makes me lie down in green pastures, he leads me beside quiet waters, He refreshes my soul.

Chapter 3

Darkness Appear

And darkness hovered over the earth; darkness was over the face of the deep *Genesis 1:2*

What is darkness? Darkness is contrast with brightness; it is a relative absence of visible light. It is the appearance of black in color space. Plato once stated that "we could forgive a child who is afraid of the dark; the real tragedy of life is when men are afraid of the light." Jesus declared to His disciples I am the light of the world. Whoever follows me will never walk in darkness but will have the light of life *John 8:12*. So it is here we find a noted fact that mankind will indeed encounter darkness.

In this chapter, we will deal with the darkness that comes after receiving your devasting news of grief. Could it be, as previously stated, death, divorce, losing a job, losing a child in a custody battle, or simply receiving any type of devastating news that will usher you into a level of grief?

From reading the first two chapters, one should have a clear understanding of how we arrived at the doorway of grief. After reading the above chapters, we all know the first thing that happens to you is a paradigm shift. In simple terms, your mindset is shifted from one reality to another reality.

We now see that the entrance of sin brings on moral decay in the world. We also understand that humans have literally shifted from good to evil and from light to darkness.

In the beginning, there was so much light. Remember, from God's hand, the man was shaped and cultivated in the light, never glimpsing at an appearance of darkness. So, every word man heard was of illumination. To illuminate means to supply or brighten with light. The light was the foundation of all of it. You see, the words that were spoken gave mankind clear direction and vision for His ordained posture of dominion and authority.

The shadow of darkness captured his being when the entrance of the deceiver showed up on the scene. Let's revisit *Genesis 3: 1-7*

Genesis 3:1-7

Now the serpent was craftier than any of the wild animals the LORD God had made. He said to the woman, "Did God really say, 'You must not eat from any tree in the garden'?"

2 The woman said to the serpent, "We may eat fruit from the trees in the garden,

3 but God did say, 'You must not eat fruit from the tree that is in the middle of the garden, and you must not touch it, or you will die.'

4 "You will not certainly die," the serpent said to the woman.

5 "For God knows that when you eat from it, your eyes will be opened, and you will be like God, knowing good and evil."

6 When the woman saw that the fruit of the tree was good for food and pleasing to the eye, and also desirable for gaining wisdom, she took some and ate it. She also gave some to her husband, who was with her, and he ate it.

7 Then the eyes of both of them were opened, and they realized they were naked; so, they sewed fig leaves together and made coverings for themselves.

It is here we find Satan assaulted our first parents to sin, and the temptation proved fatal to them. The tempter was the devil, in the shape and likeness of a serpent. Satan's plan was to draw our first parents to sin and cause separation between them and their God through the power of dark words. He set the bait with words, and he lured them in by the power of words.

Man is separated from God, which leads to the entrance of darkness to appear with words. When words were produced initially, we see the formulation of declarations and decrees being established in the earth as words of life.

A declaration is an explicit announcement, either oral or written. In the beginning, we know that the only thing released was the spoken word. Now a decree is the rule of law issued by a head of state. The question must be asked, what are the words of life? Words of life are spirit-filled; they are affirmation and power-filled words that will cause a person to be motivated to move forward and not backward. I have another question for you. Are the words that you are speaking; are they life or death? Do they give us hope or discouragement? Since we are held responsible for every word we speak, we must be mindful of the things we utter. In the book of James, every idle word that men speak he will be held accountable for. One of the disciples of Jesus knew it so well when he picked up a pen and begin to write for by thy words thou shalt be justified, and by thy words, thou shalt be condemned *Matthew 12: 36-37.*

The word justified means we are freed from all blame, we are without guilt, and we are shown or proven right. The word condemns means to pronounce unfit for use guilty. You see, it is by our own words we can be free from blame and without guilt, or we can pronounce ourselves guilty and unfit for the use of God.

There will always be gloom attached to the natural man when receiving words that will spiral them into a place of a dark night. I would like to share with you one of my dark night experiences.

Today, I remember the 3: 00am call I received from my sister when she declared come; we must go to the hospital to see about mother. Trying to get my balance together from awakening from a deep sleep, I rose from the bed and got dressed. There was no time to get made up because my sister and brother were sitting in my driveway before you knew it. When I got in the car, I stated to the angel that you must help my mother; she said, no, Johnnie, your mother is gone. I had to let the words digest and register. Still in shock, I got out of the car and walked with my sister and brother into the hospital. As we approached the security desk, I thought to myself, she will come out of this. I could remember the ride on the elevator being so long, and we were only going to the 7th floor. There was a hush in the atmosphere. We quickly walked down the corridor to her room, and there she was lying in bed lifeless, but with one glance, you would have thought she was resting or in a deep sleep. I remember the words I formulated for the nurse. My question was, she is sleeping, right? To my surprise, the nurse said in a gentle voice, no, she is gone. I stood for a moment and walked over to the bed and begin to rub her head. As the words began to resound in my head, all I could hear was no, she is gone.

Today, it has been nearly seventeen years since my mother's passing, and I understand the power of those words that were given to me during my process. To me, this was the darkest day of my life. You see, my mother stood as the one that would always be around;

she was to be the strength and backbone for the family. With her gone, what was a single woman to do? After all, it was her mother that pushed her to drive for recovery.

Thoughts kept coming. Man, I just got it together, and after all, it was my mother that had become the most consistent in my life. She was my mentor and prayer partner. All kinds of thoughts propelled through my head as I thought to myself, who will I call now; where will I go; what will I do now that mother is gone. As the shadow of darkness came and reality set in, some decisions had to be made and choices I had to choose from. I understood that the one bad mistake could push me out all the way.

The shadow of dark words always leaves the spirit of hopelessness around.

A songwriter once wrote a song:

With thoughts of hatred, I am left alone chanting the oath. I once swore my vision is blurring, stained by blood from those slain by my sword. On my knees, I lay beside them, not a single soul I can see. The shadow of darkness all around to greet me! With victory towards the light, I look with fear; I know it's not for me. I seek shelter in the dark.

It is here we see that the darkness has appeared, and hopelessness has come along simply to cage the griever into an even darker place. The griever must trust that his darkness has a light on the other side. Standing in my dark night, I am wondering what will happen next.

It was as the day stood still, and I was lost in the night, dressed only with words of hopelessness.

Man in his original state never knew hopelessness, as previously stated. The first man only knew words of light. These words help him tend to the Garden, take care of His family, and propelled him into a deeper place of worship with his creator. As sin was made known, the word is declared unto Adam and His wife you must leave Eden. This was probably one of the darkest nights of their life. At this moment, they were filled with hopelessness. As they depart from their place of beginnings, I could imagine the words of loss and gloom being rehearsed in their heads. I could see the two grievers leaving their place of security and losing all they have ever known. As they crossed over into the unknown, I am sure they crossed over having feelings of remorse, and regrets. Just as we all do as humans when we lose our footage or someone we love on the earth. All of the should-haves; and could have appeared. Today I understand that if these statements pop up. They are only appearing as alert kickers. I am to balance it out and look for blind spots that may tear up relationships meant to be covenants for a lifetime. We must be sensitive to the little things also. If we have life, then we still have opportunities to do good at all times for people and with them. It is a must we affirm our relationships by the word of God.

Adam and Eve could have stayed in a dark night for as long as they lived, but with one word, they were propelled out of their night season. I could picture Adam saying to the woman. Eve remember what our creator said! Eve, feeling depressed and sadden turning to Adam with no life, but still listening he declares the woman's seed will bruise the serpent's head. There it goes, light in a dark place shining through with one word. It is here we see Adam and Eve bursting forth to the breaking of the day.

Allow me to introduce you to another griever from the bible that was shifted into a dark night for an exceptionally long time. I bring to center stage Israel aka Jacob the griever. In reading the scriptures regarding his story, we now see this griever lost in a time capsule. The scriptures show how he saw the angels ascending and descending. He literally fought with the angel all night long. If you dig deeper into his story, you will see his struggle. The scripture indicates how Israel's dark night literally lasted for years. Causing him to miss out on many years of His life as a historical person.

Take a journey with the author and read ***Genesis Chapters 27 – 36***, and find a brief overview of what Jacob the griever missed out on:

Overview of what the griever missed out on as he experienced his type of grief:

☐ ***Genesis Chapter 27*** Jacob escapes Esau - He did not correctly bond and establish a relationship with his brother.

☐ ***Genesis Chapter 28***: his labor was hard, and he missed the wedding of Esau.

☐ ***Genesis Chapter 29***, he marries Rachael and Leah without his father and his mother being present.

☐ ***Genesis Chapter 30*** Family life not enjoyed to the fullest, labor double.

☐ ***Genesis Chapter 31*** Agreement made with Laban, Jacob flees Laban, and Laban pursues him, Laban's covenant with Jacob

☐ ***Genesis Chapter 32*** Esau comes to meet Jacob, Jacob wrestling with angels

Given Jacob and Joseph's story, we now see how a dark night lingered for many years. We also see how dark nights propel the griever into it and how it lures others connected to the griever into a night season.

Today we look at Joseph, the Dreamers father. As this griever takes center stage, his mental state is known through the words he utters in **Genesis 37: 35**.

He chose to remain in darkness by the declaration he established in his atmosphere. "He stated I shall go down into the grave to my son in mourning." His dark night was so long he missed out on many exciting things. Such as family events, weddings, the birth of grandchildren, and many other joyous occasions grieving over the thought his son Joseph was dead. What a dark night it had become for this father.

I'm now stepping into the future, knowing I have actually experienced my mother's death and the murder of my brother. I would like to let you know; a dark night should be considered a birthing room for one's transition in life. To me, dark nights should be considered a classroom with a pupil with no teacher's vision.

So, it is in the natural; it is in the spirit. The darkest hour always appears before the dawn. Dark nights are classrooms set up by God's supernatural hand to propel the griever into the unknown, to birth wisdom and maturity.

On a dark night, you lose your ability to see, constantly stumbling and never finding your way out. When the griever begins to recognize that he no longer has a vision for tomorrow; it is in that moment reality will set in. They will begin to have a clear understanding that they cannot and will not make it through the night alone. Job declared it like this, in the day of my trouble, I sought the Lord; in the night, my hand was stretched out without wearying: my soul refused to be comforted ***Psalms 77:2*** NIV. He was literally saying that I am wounded, and I cannot come up and out of this alone. I will hold on to you without throwing in the towel. It's not over until you bring me out. Job declared that he was weak, but His God was big enough to carry him over into the day! He became dependent upon the strength of the creator, the All-Sufficient One. To be dependent means you are relying on something or someone else for aid or support.

As you become dependent on The Almighty, a ray of light will burst forth. This will be a clear indicator that you are on the right path. As I pen this paper now, I could hear my mother saying hush; the birds are talking to God. I want to arise from the night and talk to the father.

Words, they are so powerful! To the griever, what will you hear as night swiftly approaches? Will you hear they are gone but will live again, or will you allow yourself to be dressed in the power of words that will cripple your moment in the earth! I don't think your loved one would want that. So as your night season comes and the words resound, remember you are walking through the valley, and there are ditches there for you.

Let us look within and start from here using our words wisely and allow them to be spirit-filled with power. I could imagine you are saying to yourself now, what! How do I start, and where do I begin? It's easy. The

Word of God is Spirit and Life, so what better way to start dressing yourself. Get yourself a Bible, take one verse of scripture, and declare it over your life for one month. Memorize it and then walk it out.

Let's try one together, and at the end of this book, I want you to make a declaration over someone's life living under the shadow of darkness.

Below you will find your covenant of agreement to memorize the scripture and declare it daily for a month. Sign the agreement and indicate the name of the person you have agreed to speak words of light over.

Chapter 4

Where Is Hope

Now faith is the evidence of what we hope for and the assurance about what we do not see.

Hebrews 11:1

Quotes: To hope is to risk pain. To try is to risk failure, but risk must be taken because the greatest hazard in life is to risk nothing,

Quotes: "Many of the greatest achievements of the world were accomplished by tired and discouraged men who kept moving."

As we open up this chapter, I want to deal with being opened up from the night. We have gone through

The following steps of the griever:

• Understanding the entrance of the death syndrome

• What happens when the griever receives the initial word of lost

- Moving into denial as you accept the night season

As the author opens this chapter, she wanted to give the reader something to think about. She wanted to open you up to the world of hope. To have hope means you have an existence. To have no hope is like a ship without a sail. Apostle Paul put it like this when he wrote to the Corinthian Church "Therefore, we do not lose heart. Even though our outward man is perishing, yet the inward man is renewed day by day. For our light affliction which is but for a moment; is working for us a far more exceeding and eternal weight of glory. While we do not look at the things that are seen, they are not seen. For the things which are seen are temporary, but the things which are not eternal.

II Corinthians 4:16-18.

Apostle Paul wanted the Corinthian church to understand that he did have hope, and it was working even when he could see he was bound in chains. Locked behind prison walls, he shared his hopes and His dreams of being free in the spirit.

As the griever, you must ask yourself several questions. What have I bound today that will paralyze me from moving forward? Who or what is causing me to faint and lose hope? To be faint means, you are weak, dizzy, and likely to collapse. It is a breakdown in vital energy, strength, or stamina. It is a state of extreme prostration and physical depression.

As I pen this page, my mind reflects back to the prophet Isaiah. Isaiah was known as the eagle eye prophet. He had 20/20 vision in the spirit. One must note that the eagle eye prophets grew faint from time to time. Isaiah prophesied to a people that had lost all hope. His prophecy was full of life as he began to tell Israel to Awake and arise. Isaiah told them to wake up! He repeated himself several times. He declared O Zion! Clothe yourself with strength. Put on your beautiful clothes. Oh, holy city of Jerusalem, for unclean and godless people will enter your gates no longer. *Isaiah 52:1*. It is so crucial for the griever to realize that all hope is not gone.

Isaiah knew the moral decay and hopelessness of the people. He wanted them to take courage and realize that there would be hope as long as there was life. When life is gone, the ability to have hope fades away. Why? Because there is no future existence. Israel was grieved because they realized they had failed their God. While failing their God, they mingled with the uncircumcised and became captive to other Gods. Deeper and more profound in sin, they propelled, and the chains of captivity could be heard. Grieved in spirit with lost hope, Isaiah stood before a stiff neck people and began prophesying hope. Having an eagle eye, he knew within their spirit hope lay dormant because of their lifestyle. He declared the spirit of the Sovereign Lord upon me because the Lord has anointed me to preach good news to the poor. He has sent me to bind up the brokenhearted, to proclaim freedom for the captives and release from darkness for the prisoners.

Isaiah 61:1.

The author believes that what Isaiah did was ignite what was already within the people. Anointed by God, he saw beyond their grief and spoke to their spirit to quicken what was buried.

Indeed, underneath the surface of grief was the treasure of hope that had to be awakened. As the seed of hope was awakened, Isaiah then declared that God would give a crown of beauty for ashes and a joyous blessing instead of mourning to all who mourn in Israel. This would be a powerful exchange.

So now it is time for the griever to deal with the spirit of hopelessness. It is incredible how you could be filled with so much hope in one moment, and in the next second, all hope is gone. This could be described as the yo-yo syndrome to those who view these situations from the outside who have never experienced grief. The Yo-Yo Syndrome is the up and down mood cycle. The primary factor in this syndrome is the emotions of the griever. What are emotions? Emotions are a mental state that arises spontaneously rather than through conscious effort and is often accompanied by physiological changes. It is a state of mental agitation or disturbance. It is the part that involves sensibility. To the reader, please understand that the seat of our emotions is linked to the heart. One of my sister s stated that nowadays, the source of emotion and passion is considered the heart, poetically referring to the soul and physically tied to the feeling of love. You see, when grief is introduced, your heart feels as if it has been shattered and so you become connected to the shadow of hopelessness.

I used to hear my mother say, "that a man who has no hope is a man most miserable." To be miserable is to be wretchedly unhappy or uncomfortable. She would then say, "misery loves company." So, I say to the griever, don't allow your hopelessness to wear you out. If you let hopelessness come in, you should expect his kindred brother misery to tag along also. These two spirits are dangerous. They will spiral the griever into another level of darkness.

Allow me to testify a little. We had never been this way before. I declare I was miserable, and those that were connected probably felt that same miserable spirit. Nevertheless, we continued on with what we had to take care of. Early in the morning, we all knew we had to go meet with the funeral undertaker and didn't know what to expect. As we awaken that morning after crying and sleeplessness. We gathered together at the meeting destination. All seven siblings and aunts, and uncles gather into the room as we begin to prepare for my mother's funeral. A lot of talking was going on in the room, but it felt like I was in a dark corner. As I awoke from my hopelessness, I remembered the undertaker asking, "did my mother have insurance?" We each looked at one another, and I remembered and declared, oh yes, I have a policy for her. The silence was broken, and I remember walking out of the office and getting into our several cars. We all gather back at mother's house to speak about our next steps. I could remember seeing my grandfather as he rolled up to my mother's house. In my head, I said, "what parent outlives his child"? But all I could literally do was hug him as he prepared to enter mother's home with his handkerchief in his hand, rubbing his eyes. Talking about hopelessness, this took the case. It is something tragic when a parent hears of the death of a child.

Many parents have experienced the shock of waking up to find their child dead. One moment the child is healthy and happy, and the next minute they are gone. I am reminded of a man in the bible who lost his firstborn. He was lost and had no hope for his future. I must allow David to take center stage and testify. Take a journey with the author to the book of Samuel.

Read *II Samuel 12:1-31* with me. (visit biblegateway.com or grab your bible, and let's read the text h before you read the next paragraph).

In this passage, we see the griever David mourning over His son's loss because of His sins, but we also see him muster up enough strength to worship.

The scripture declares in verses 20-31, David arose from the earth washed, anointed himself, and changed his apparel. He then came into the house of the Lord and worshipped: then he came to his own house; and when he required, they set bread before him, and he did eat. Then said the servant unto him, What thing is this that thou hast did? Thou didst fast and weep for the child, while it was alive, but when the child was dead, thou didst rise and eat bread. And he said, while the child was yet alive, I fasted and wept: for I said, who can tell whether God will be gracious to me, that the child may live. But now he is dead, wherefore should I fast? Can I bring him back again? I shall go to him, but he shall not return to me.

Because of the above scripture, we see David the mourner faint at heart because of his son's death. He had lost all hope but realized it was vital for him to do several things. First, he washed and changed his apparel. Secondly, he worshipped. As we look at David and

Bathsheba's loss, one would say this was a terrible thing for a family to encounter.

In these particular verses, we see the loss of hope and strength through the power of worship. Often, the griever finds himself losing hope and wanting to crawl up in a cave to be isolated. It is in this time the griever desires are to be left alone and uncared for. By shrinking back, the griever will sometimes retreat to not washing or changing their apparel. The author would suggest this moment should be considered as the I Don't Care Syndrome. This syndrome simply means nothing, or no one really matters.

The griever must try to avoid this syndrome. This syndrome has a crippling effect. To be cripple means you are physically disabled, and you are unable to move. It is the enemy's job to cancel out every good and perfect plan of God for your life. If the griever becomes isolated, then the gateway is open for major depression to set in. I want to declare unto you the devil is a liar, and you shall come up and out.

David showed the griever a perfect example of losing hope and regaining the momentum in the spirit. One must prophetically look at the movement of David by the spirit as he grieved. He went in with His strength, but when he came out, it was the strength of God that made him stand with hope again.

Let's view the stages of David once again:
• The First Thing he did was wash and change his apparel

To define the wash means to be made clean. It is the act or process of removing a stain or removal of something that should not be. Daily we understand that God wants to cleanse us. The writer in Psalms 51:7 declared that if the Lord washed him, he would be made whiter than snow. Psalms 51:7. David declared in Psalms that he wanted God to create a clean heart and renew the right spirit within him. Then only would he be white as snow.

Apparel – is a covering or adornment, a garment.
• The Second Thing he did was He Worshipped Reverent honor and homage paid to God

The act of referencing

As David began to change his apparel, he was preparing to worship in a grieving state. So, as it is in the natural, it is in the spirit. As the griever comes to the Lord broken, a great exchange will literally take place in the spirit.

Matthew 11:28-29 declares, come unto me all ye who are weary and are heavily laden, and I will give you rest. Take my yoke upon you and learn of me; for I am meek and lowly in heart, and ye shall find rest unto your souls. As the griever begins to worship in spirit and truth, great transformation will occur through the spirit. They will begin to be lifted to a place of tranquility. A place where tears fall, and a cup is there to catch them.

What the griever must understand is their walk of grief is a walk that must be processed. It must be walked out with the creator. Therefore, you must be honest and genuine with yourself with your answers. The griever must understand they will be the only one coming out, and as they come out, they will want their liberation to bless others that will be walking through the grief process.

Daily Disciplines for the Griever
Closing out this chapter

Steps to avoid the I Don't Care Syndrome

1. Create a daily prayer time
2. Meditate on the word
3. Make small, positive changes
4. Banish negative thinking
5. Look at the beautiful side of things
6. Exercise
7. Appreciate loved ones
8. Pursue a passion
9. Talk and work with other excited people
10. Take time to recharge
11. Get great feedback
12. Help Others

Yo-Yo Syndrome

1. Examine yourself to see if you are suffering from the Yo-Yo Syndrome? What is this syndrome? You wear your emotions on your shoulder.

Daily Seek to be a True Worshipper

The fact is true worship is not defined by a place, a feeling, or a ritual. God sets the standards for true worship in His Word, and his standard is much higher and more rewarding than most of us could imagine.

Simply remember, true worship is a whole life response to God's greatness and glory. One who worship by spirit and truth.

Chapter 5

Cup of Tears

He will wipe every tear from their eyes. There will be no more death or mourning or crying or pain, for the old order of things will be passed away.

Now that you have read the first four chapters of this book, you should understand that the griever has a process that they must walkthrough. What does the word process mean? It is a natural progressively continuing operation or development marked by a series of gradual changes. We see that the griever can, in fact, stay in one stage for a lengthy period of time. Every griever that walks through this process; must walk through at their own pace, and with each step, they will be ushered into a new time.

What is time? It is the indefinite continued progress of existence and events in the past, present, and future regarded as a whole. Time is a part of the measuring system used to sequence events, compare the duration of events and intervals between them, and quantify rates of change such as object motions. The temporal present is continually changing; events happen and are located further and further in the past. Time has been a significant subject of religion, philosophy, and science, but defining it in a manner applicable to all fields of study without circularity eluded scholars. A simple definition states that time is what a clock measure.

Something to think about, right! While you are thinking, ask yourself this question? Who holds your past, present, and future?

Today I would like to clarify to the reader that the creator of all things is the time holder and timekeeper. I believe that every second of time is in the hands of the creator. Because God has created all things, He knows what is required for the existence of all things, including the seasons of it.

Allow me to introduce you to another griever by the name of Solomon. Solomon is declared to be one of the wisest and wealthiest men that ever lived. Even wise men grieve. As a king, I am sure that Solomon had to walk through many difficult periods during his tenure. I believe it was in those dark moments of his life; tears fell, and grief overtook his very being. Coming up, I never imagined, out of tears, a hush came over his spirit. He began to pick up the pen. With his eyes being filled with tears, he began to decree that to everything under the heavens, there were time, purpose, and seasons attached to our lives.

Ecclesiastes 3:1

The king was literally saying that this circumstance of grief will only last for a moment, but we must learn the lessons that will be presented.

He understood that even though there was darkness, dawn would soon appear. I went to my concordance to see what the testimony of *Ecclesiastes 3* would be: 1-10, and Matthew Henry put it like this:

To expect endless happiness in a changing world must end in disappointment. To bring ourselves to our state in life is our duty in wisdom in this world. God's whole plan for the world's government will be found altogether wise, just, and good. Then let us seize the favorable opportunity for every good purpose and work. The time to die is fast approaching. Thus, labor and sorrow fill the world. This is given us that we may always have something to do; none was sent into this world to be idle. Both of these men were literally saying that it was fulfilling what you were created to do and do it with passion. Because when your time here on planted earth has passed by, you will literally never see it again. They both understood that tears would be shed, and they would sometimes cloud their view, but joy would come in the morning.

A songwriter wrote:

Baby, can you stop the rain from falling? Won't you chase my clouds away? I'd give anything to see the sun again. Only you can stop these tears from falling. I can't face another day. Can you stop the rain? The songwriter's whisper is of rain, but he suggests to the listener he had tears from a broken heart. So, his request was for someone to make his tears stop. He decided enough was enough with free will, and he didn't want to cry anymore.

What are tears? It's a drop of clear saline fluid secreted by the lacrimal gland and diffused between the eyes and eyelids to moisten the parts and facilitate their motion. Many people associated tears with sorrow, but I beg to differ. There are many forms of tears. Let's view a few below:

Tears of Joy

To cry when you are made happy or made glad. This emotion is evoked by well-being, success, or good fortune.

Tears of Sorrow

To cry because of deep distress caused by loss, disappointment, or other misfortune suffered by oneself or others.

Tear of Grief

Crying because of deep sorrow esp. that caused by someone's death. Trouble or annoyance

Crocodile Tears

An Insincere display of false crying

Tears of Hopelessness

Cry because you have no expectation of good or success. Crying because you are not susceptible to remedy.

Tears of Fear

Is the act of crying when a distressing emotion is aroused by impending danger, evil, or pain.

After reading different forms of tears, the reader is now permitted to come in agreement with the author and declare there are many forms of tears.

Today the author would like you to take a journey with her as we look at the "Cup of Tears" shed by the griever. I could remember as a child, my sisters and I lived in the project, and the windows were really high. I was nine, and the younger two were eight and six. When it rains, we couldn't go outside because my mom wouldn't allow it. So, we would play near the window in the front room and say, rain, rain, go away, come again another day. We were told that God was crying for the world we lived in. As children, we felt horrible that God was crying for his creation. Why should he cry when he made it all?

Now that I am older, I understand the prophetic message. If indeed God cried, it was because the human race failed and continually fails to receive His message of love. As children, we were telling the rain to stop so that we could go out to play. Literally, we used the power of words. We spoke into our atmosphere and shifted the elements for us to go and take our posture.

In the realm of the spirit, as I revisit those words, rain, rain goes away come again another day. Today as I connect this word to the griever, it is imperative the griever allow His faith to speak to every element that isolates him. It is a must they speak the words of life that will produce a highway to their cave or isolated place. Standing with tears of grief, the cave will be opened for them to assume the position to become the healed of the Lord.

Come now, allow me to introduce you to two other grievers' from the Bible by Mary and Martha's name. Mary was known as the worshipper, and Martha was the one that had the Ministry of Helps. Martha was always in the spotlight working her stuff, and Mary she was the one that simply wanted to hear and worship. To the reader, I want you to understand that death will knock on everyone's door. You now see how a worshipper and the team ministry leader are hit by the spirit of grief. This story is found in all the gospels, but today let us view it from the beloved John's eyes.

John 11: 1-48

Now a man named Lazarus was sick. He was from Bethany, the village of Mary and her sister Martha.

2 (This Mary, whose brother Lazarus now lay sick, was the same one who poured perfume on the Lord and wiped his feet with her hair.)

3 So the sisters sent word to Jesus, "Lord, the one you love is sick."

4 When he heard this, Jesus said, "This sickness will not end in death. No, it is for God's glory so that God's Son may be glorified through it."

5 Now Jesus loved Martha and her sister and Lazarus.

6 So when he heard that Lazarus was sick, he stayed where he was two more days,

7 and then he said to his disciples, "Let us go back to Judea."

8 "But Rabbi," they said, "a short while ago the Jews there tried to stone you, and yet you are going back?"

9 Jesus answered, "Are there not twelve hours of daylight? Anyone who walks in the daytime will not stumble, for they see by this world's light.

10 It is when a person walks at night that they stumble, for they have no light."

11 After he had said this, he went on to tell them, "Our friend Lazarus has fallen asleep; but I am going there to wake him up."

12 His disciples replied, "Lord, if he sleeps, he will get better."

13 Jesus had been speaking of his death, but his disciples thought he meant natural sleep.

14 So then he told them plainly, "Lazarus is dead,

15 and for your sake I am glad I was not there, so that you may believe. But let us go to him."

16 Then Thomas (also known as Didymus[a]) said to the rest of the disciples, "Let us also go, that we may die with him."

17 On his arrival, Jesus found that Lazarus had already been in the tomb for four days.

18 Now Bethany was less than two miles[b] from Jerusalem,

19 and many Jews had come to Martha and Mary to comfort them in the loss of their brother.

20 When Martha heard that Jesus was coming, she went out to meet him, but Mary stayed at home.

21 "Lord," Martha said to Jesus, "if you had been here, my brother would not have died.

22 But I know that even now God will give you whatever you ask."

23 Jesus said to her, "Your brother will rise again."

24 Martha answered, "I know he will rise again in the resurrection at the last day."

25 Jesus said to her, "I am the resurrection and the life. The one who believes in me will live, even though they die;

26 and whoever lives by believing in me will never die. Do you believe this?"

27 "Yes, Lord," she replied, "I believe that you are the Messiah, the Son of God, who is to come into the world."

28 After she had said this, she went back and called her sister Mary aside. "The Teacher is here," she said, "and is asking for you."

29 When Mary heard this, she got up quickly and went to him.

30 Now Jesus had not yet entered the village but was still at the place where Martha had met him.

31 When the Jews who had been with Mary in the house, comforting her, noticed how quickly she got up and went out, they followed her, supposing she was going to the tomb to mourn there.

32 When Mary reached the place where Jesus was and saw him, she fell at his feet and said, "Lord, if you had been here, my brother would not have died."

33 When Jesus saw her weeping, and the Jews who had come along with her also weeping, he was deeply moved in spirit and troubled.

34 "Where have you laid him?" he asked.

"Come and see, Lord," they replied.

35 Jesus wept.

36 Then the Jews said, "See how he loved him!"

37 But some of them said, "Could not he who opened the eyes of the blind man have kept this man from dying?"

38 Jesus, once more deeply moved, came to the tomb. It was a cave with a stone laid across the entrance.

39 "Take away the stone," he said.

"But, Lord," said Martha, the sister of the dead man, "by this time there is a bad odor, for he has been there four days."

40 Then Jesus said, "Did I not tell you that if you believe, you will see the glory of God?"

41 So they took away the stone. Then Jesus looked up and said, "Father, I thank you that you have heard me.

42 I knew that you always hear me, but I said this for the benefit of the people standing here, that they may believe that you sent me."

43 When he had said this, Jesus called in a loud voice, "Lazarus, come out!"

44 The dead man came out, his hands and feet wrapped with strips of linen, and a cloth around his face.

Jesus said to them, "Take off the grave clothes and let him go."

45 Therefore many of the Jews who had come to visit Mary, and had seen what Jesus did, believed in him.

46 But some of them went to the Pharisees and told them what Jesus had done.

47 Then the chief priests and the Pharisees called a meeting of the Sanhedrin.

"What are we accomplishing?" they asked. "Here is this man performing many signs.

48 If we let him go on like this, everyone will believe in him, and then the Romans will come and take away both our temple and our nation."

Indeed, both sisters were affected, and they both responded in different manners. Their tears were an outpour of built-up emotions. These emotions could have been anger, bitterness, sorrow, joy, fear, but nevertheless, these emotions were locked up inside and had to find a way of escape.

It is here we see a different side of a worshipper affected by grief. Mary was always so humble. After all, she was the one that sat at Jesus' feet. I could see Mary now standing at his tomb, shedding tears of sorrow and tears of grief. What a horrific state to be in. You just read what the different types of tears were, so now imagine her spirit mixed with the two. With a loss for words, all she could do was let her tears fall into a cup, knowing that her lifeless brother laid in a tomb.

On the other hand, Martha, still mourning and crying for the loss of her brother with tears streaming down her face declared unto Jesus when he arrived, "If you had been here, my brother would not have died." Sounds like anger and rage to me. Mary, on the other hand, simply stayed calm.

Given the writer's perception, grievers will respond differently. Allow the author to testify for a moment regarding her cup of tears.

Let us revisit the story of the author's brother tragedy. It has been ten years since my brother departed this life. His death was premature and unexpected. This tragedy was something my family never expected, but every moment became a reality. My brother was robbed and beaten, as stated earlier. One moment he was alive, and the next moment he was on the machine. I could remember going to the hospital daily for 4 days, reading healing scriptures, and holding his hands. I also remembered when he was transported over to UMD Hospital to have surgery. My family sat in the room awaiting the news of his recovery. We went home even though he was not moved and changed our attire. When arriving back at the hospital, we were told we had to make decisions. I could remember standing in the corridor with my niece asking the question, how do you think your father would want to live. My heart was heavy. After all, Minister McCall was my roommate. Tears flowed down my face even when I tried to be strong for my nieces. These tears were something that I could not hide. These tears were my emotions speaking louder than my voice.

It is said that eyes are the window to one's soul. On the day that my brother departed this life, my soul was speaking loud and clear. As I stood in the room and watch him take his last breath, I believe the cup was extended from heaven for every one of our tears. The room was filled with weeping and groaning, and not one eye was dry simply because tears are connected to the heart.

Many would say to see a man cry is a sign of weakness. I beg to differ. If you see a man cry, he will be showing you his strength. It is when we hide our emotions we become cowardly. A coward lacks the courage to do or endure dangerous or unpleasant things. Like Mary, Martha, and the author cry, if you must for it will be in the process of crying, your sorrow will be turned into joy, and the shadow of hope will once again appear.

As time swiftly fades away today, I want the griever to understand that tears are a part of their process. So, if you must cry, cry, but pick yourself up and don't allow yourself to stay in a low place. Square your shoulders and began to declare this too shall pass.

A Songwriter was in a sad state at one point in his life and begins to pen these words. I can see clearly now that the rain is gone. I could see all obstacles in my way. Now that the dark cloud has passed me by, it's going to be a bright, bright sunshiny day. It's going to be a bright sunshiny day.

The griever must understand the amount of time he stays in this stage is up to him. When mankind was created, He was given free will, the will to do, and become. In simple terminology, he was given the authority to do as he will. He was given the liberty to make choices. You see, it will be your choice to stand with the gloomy cloud or awaken to sunshine with tears that will eventually turn to joy.

Allow the author to help you along your way by starting your day with a declaration. Below you will find a declaration that will boost you forward.

Let's make a declaration over our lives now:

I decree and declare the light of God is operating in me and through me. As stated in *Matthew 5:14*, I am the light of the world that city cannot be hidden. Today, I decree that I will exchange tears of sorrow for the release of tears of joy, and the joy of the Lord shall be my strength. I confess now that all things shall work together for my good, and no negative seed shall uproot the good. I decree and declare that I shall be like the tree planted by the rivers of living waters that can and will not be moved. On this day, I will operate in dominion and power. Nothing shall be missing, nothing shall be announced broken, and I will have all that I require because the hand of God is with me. I decree and declare the angel of the Lord goes before me to bring me into that prepared place.

THINGS TO REMEMBER

Signs of Revealed hopelessness to Watch Out for

1. Alienation

Refers to estrangement, emotional isolation, or dissociation, the act of being alone, a state of being an outsider, or the feeling of being isolated, as from society.

2. Forsakenness

Completely deserted or helpless; abandoned

3. Uninspired

Lacking in imagination or originality, not filled with excitement

4. Powerlessness

Devoid of strength or resources; lacking the authority or capacity to act. Lacking strength or power; helpless and total ineffectual

5. Oppression

The exercise of authority or power in a burdensome, cruel or unjust manner.

6. Limitedness

Confined or restricted within certain limits. Not attaining the highest goal or achievement

7. Doom

A decision of judgment, it's over; finality

8. Captivity

Imprisonment o hostage: the state of being confined to a space

9. Helplessness

Unable to help oneself, powerless or incompetent.

Lacking support or protection

Chapter 6

The Shadow of Hope

As we open up this chapter, I would like to rehearse what we have just read regarding the griever process. Thus far, we have gone over:

• Understanding the entrance of the death syndrome

• Receiving the initial word

• Moving into denial as you accept the night season

• Having a sense of hopelessness

• The Season of tears

As the author continues to journey with you, she would like to shed some awareness on this next phase for the griever. This stage deals with shadows. Shadows can be a little tricky at times. Because it deals with seeing but not really facing what you see. Let us look at what a shadow is.

A shadow is an area where direct light from a light source cannot reach due to an object's obstruction. Another dictionary says it is the rough image cast by an object blocking rays of illumination. It could be an area that is not or is only partially irradiated or illuminated because of interception of radiation by an opaque object between the area and the source of radiation. So, you see the reality of a shadow, the matter is here, but there is some type of blockage of the reality of the real deal. What does the word blockage mean? It is an obstruction that makes movement or flows difficult or impossible. If we were to pause now and do a survey, 99% out of 100 of my readers could confess that they had a blockage at one point in their life. Something to think about, right! At this point of the process, you are almost ready to cross over your hurdle, but just like a runner when he is training, something always gets in the way.

Another example would be a person with Coronary Artery Disease. This person's blockage could be so bad it literally snaps the life away from him. In the natural, so it is in the spirit for the person that grieves having a shadow of hope is not good enough. You want to have the appearance of it. If the reader has noticed, the stages before this one was hard to break free from. If, in fact, the griever has made it to this point, a breakthrough is right around the corner. I could remember as a child those long-extended vacations in the summer. Not really realizing that these moments were considered breaks for my mother. It was 7 of us, and then she adopted a foster child. At first, when we would pile into my aunts' car, we would all be so happy.

To this day, I still don't remember how we all got into that little station wagon. The first 3 days away from home were great, but I wanted to go home when the excitement died. On those long nights, I remember auntie saying, alright, it's 7pm time to hit the sack. Back at home, we really didn't have to get in bed that early. I thought auntie was the meanest woman on the planet.

Living in the projects was a little different. We had 5 bedrooms, kitchen, living room, and bathroom all on the same level at my Aunt's house. It was different she had upstairs and downstairs. I would hate to go to bed because I use to hear the sound of shoes coming up the stairs at night. Because I sleep near the door, I would see shadows, and these shadows would literally scare the life out of me because I could not see the real deal. I could remember one night, as the shadow approached the top stairs, I jumped over my baby sisters and went under the bed. There we took our abode and slept the entire night because of the fear of a shadow.

To the griever, because of the above story, shadows can be frightening if you don't know a thing's reality. Once you have stayed in grief and sorrow for some time, what appears to be hope simply appears to be fear. I once heard Pastor Roderick Allen declare that fear was false evidence appearing real. Sounds like a shadow to me. You must face your reality and come up and out from the shadow of fear. It wasn't until the following day my sisters and I decided to come from under the bed at daybreak.

To the griever, you must know that since you passed through the other stages of your grief process, the breaking of day is here. Once you grab hold of your fear, you will begin to take charge of your day with the power at work in you. A songwriter once wrote these words:

Looks like I can feel the breaking of day. Oh, what joy breaking forth in my soul. Now I've been down so long I could not hear a song, darkness covered up my head, and I felt like I was dead. I had sunk so low in sin I thought I'll never see the light again. But thank God he passed my way, and I can feel the breaking of day.

How joyful it must be to come from under the shadow and see a burst of light. Let's follow the author. She allows another griever from the bible to take center stage to show us how shadows of darkness cover's the honest truth. Come now, allow me to introduce you to a man called Isaac.

Genesis 27: 1-46, let us grab our bibles or simply go to Biblegateway.com to view scripture together.

How sad the account of this griever? The man Isaac had literally grown old, and his eyes were fading. In fact, he saw shadows. We see he saw from a shadow and was tricked into blessing the wrong son with blurred vision. When operating under the shadow, we see it is easy to be misguided by others. Your inner spirit is always in tune and ready for discernment to speak out, but the shadow will try to silence it. We see how Isaac 8-22 discernment was kicking in, but the flesh outweighs when he touch the hair on his neck and arm because of the scripture text. The griever must be sensitive to those they incorporate into their life because living in the shadow, manipulation will always show up.

It is essential to realize that you have a hiding place as you are coming up and out of your current state. David knew it so well when he declared in Psalms 91 whoever dwells in the shelter of the Most High will rest in the shadow of the almighty. I will say of the Lord, He is my refuge and my fortress, my God, in whom I trust.

As the griever is ushered out, they will finally find renewed strength and hope. Isaiah said in 40:31 yet, the strength of those who wait with hope in the Lord will be renewed. They will soar on wings like eagles. They will walk and won't grow tired. To be renewed is to resume (an activity) after an interruption. To be reestablished. So, to the griever, are you ready to run now? It is a must you come up and out of the shadow, for your hope will ignite the others that grieve.

Chapter 7

Hope Beyond Tears

I used to hear my mother say," for every valley, there is a mountain. For every mountain, there shall be a valley" What she was saying was the high places will be brought low, and the low place shall be exalted.

My mother learned to stand strong because of the contrary winds of life. As a child, I could remember in 1968, she received the call that her mother was rushed to the Jersey City Medical Center. My mother rushed from the Barrow Street apartment to her mother's bedside. Standing at the bedside, she watched her mother take her last breath. For years I would see my mother cry holding her mother's picture, but I never saw her go under. My mother grieved for so long I literally thought her tears would never stop. Some days you would hear her say, I sure do miss my mother.

As years went by, my mother found a local church and begin to pray earnestly and slowly, but surely you would see a wounded heart healed. It wasn't until I opened my eyes that I recognized her tears had faded away. It takes courage to face a brand-new day, and somehow Mother Mary obtained the inner strength to continue on. When her children were in trouble, and she required an issue to be resolved, she would drop to her knees and declare this too shall pass!

Because of the above testimony, the griever must understand that grief's pain will come with ease with time and proper care. The griever must come to grip that every time the news of death arises, it will open their hearts up with the memory of their loss. When the thought of their loss reappears, they cherish memories and appreciate the legacy the individual has left behind. Many have gone on, but their voices are still heard and echoed in the earth by a husband, wife, sister, brother, aunt, or uncle.

The author paints a good picture of the griever and allows them to see an impression of what was left behind and always remember losing their loved one.

As we come to a close but not an end, the author would like to declare that there is hope beyond your tears. It is now March 2021. It will be 18 years that my mother has been gone; for my brother, it has only been 10 years, but I declare it feels like yesterday. I thought that after my mother's death, I would never get a second wind, but to my surprise, I am still standing by the grace of God, for there is hope beyond our tears. Still standing with grace, I continued to come up, but I was hit with an unexpected blow. Like a boxer in a ring, blow by blow, I accept the hits, going down only to rise up again. Indeed, there is hope beyond our tears.

The author would like to introduce her final biblical griever to center stage. This griever shows up on the scene as one of Jesus' disciples. He was a part of the elite crew better known as a part of the inner circle of Jesus. His name was Peter, better known as quickdraw and aka the denier. He was the one that declared, I will lay my life down for you. Jesus came back and told him, really, before the rooster crows, you will deny me three times.

Come let us now journey with the author to the book John to see the account of this griever:
John 13: 1-38, 18;15-28; 20;1-30; 21:1-25

Now let us view the text; in our opening story. We see our griever positioning himself to grieve even before his leader's death by his actions. It is here we find Peter taking center stage at the last supper and Jesus predicting his betrayal. At this point, all of the disciples felt grief; they all thought within themselves, oh no, not me. Jesus knowing all things declared, I am telling you now before it happens, so that when it does happen, you will believe that I am who I am. He went on to declare, I tell you, whoever accepts anyone I send accepts me, and whoever accepts me accepts the one who sent me. After he said this, Jesus was troubled in spirit and testified. Very truly, I tell you, one of you is going to betray me. I could image all around the room the hush in the atmosphere and in the heads of the disciples, them pondering on which one of them would be the one that would do this wicked thing.

The scripture indicates that the disciples stared at one another, at a loss to know which of them he meant. One of them, the disciple whom Jesus loved, was reclining next to him. Peter motioned to this disciple and said, ask him which one he means." Peter was of the inner circle, and he knew that if a question were asked, the Rabbi would answer. The story goes on, and Jesus gives an answer.

So, Jesus then declared to the pointed one what you are about to do; do it quickly. Jesus continued releasing a word to the disciple about his departure. Our griever broke in the middle of his conversation and declared I will go with you. Jesus then declares, where I am going, you cannot follow now, but you will follow later. Peter then asked why I can't follow you now. I will lay down my life for you. At this moment, Jesus began to declare, will you really lay down your life for me? He went on to proclaim that Peter the griever would deny him not once but three times. Peter, not knowing the future, did not know what was to be. I could see him continuing on never really thinking about the word that was released unto him in shock.

Allow the author to pause for a moment and share this with you; how often was a word predicted to you, and you never meditated on it and took it to heart? Think about it?

The author wants to interject that your spirit should be discerning enough to weigh words out. If we would meditate on some of the words we received from others, we could avoid many pitfalls and mistakes. I used to hear my mother say why you would hit your head on a rock if you see the person before you do it. She was saying she was learning from others' mistakes so you will not feel the effects they did.

Given Peter's story, he showed us a lesson to be learned, as Mother would have stated. "Never say what you will not do because you will never know until you get to that moment. Peter, not really paying attention to the words because of fear, sinking deeper into a place of denial and grief. How filled with grief his days had become; his nights were long, and his heart was so heavy because his teacher was gone, and he felt like he could never make up for his denial to him.

So, what he does is go to the place where he could find solace. What is solace? It is a place of comfort or consolation of distress or sadness. Peter got around those that would love him and those that had his well-being at heart.

Often times the griever wants to seclude to a place of isolation to shrink back from the reality of their grief. Still, it is in those very moments you must surround yourself with those that will love you back to life. Peter knew it oh so well he found his way back to His brothers (disciples). There he would also find Mary, Martha, Lazarus, and the inner circle of Jesus. These individuals would reaffirm who he was called to be.

As we continue with the story of our griever by the name of Peter, we found that an empty tomb is introduced as he listens to Mary Magdalene's words. This could have been his breaking point, but it didn't break him. This griever had to see for himself that his teacher was not in the tomb. As he enters the tomb, he bent over he saw the strips of linen lying there. As well as the cloth that had been wrapped around Jesus' head. The cloth was still lying in its place, separate from the linen. When the other disciples arrived, I could imagine tears rolling down Peter's face as he gazed upon the others. So overtaken with grief, they still did not understand from scripture that Jesus had to rise from the dead.

The disciples went back to where they were staying. Full of grief, I could imagine them still saying, "where is the body of our Lord"? It is here Peter and the others are left with their thoughts and pain. How long their day must have been. Grief has a tendency to be dragged out for long periods. It could literally feel like there are 48 hours in 1 day when we all know that there are only 24 hours to it.

As our story continues, tears are fading as the angels meet Mary at the tomb and declare Jesus has risen. Mary begins to see beyond her tears the hope for all mankind.

Mary then goes to testify to the disciples of the appearance of her Lord. Talking about Hope beyond the tears, her excitement showed it. Still, gloomy Peter and the others gather together in the evening of that first day of the week and what they hoped for they actually saw. Jesus appeared before them, and they were overjoyed. He declared peace be unto you; it was those words that brought hope for their tomorrow.

I want you to understand that death is gain for those who depart this life to the griever in reality. Apostle Paul puts it like this in his letter to the Corinthian Church. Yes, we are fully confident, and we would rather be away from these earthly bodies, for then we will be at home with the Lord.

II Corinthians 5:8 NLT.

The believer is well assured by faith that there is another happy life after this is ended, but he has good hope. Through grace, heaven is a dwelling-place, a resting-place, and a hiding-place. In our Father's house, there are many mansions whose Builder and Maker is God.

The happiness of the future state is what God has prepared for those that love him: everlasting habitations, not like the earthly tabernacles, the poor cottage of clay, in which our souls now dwell; that are moldering and decaying whose foundations are in the dust.

The body of flesh is a heavy burden; the calamities of life are a heavy load. Believers groan, being burdened with a body of sin, and because of many corruptions remaining and raging within them. Death will strip us of clothing of flesh and all the comforts of life, as well as end our troubles here below. Indeed, the author paints a vivid picture for you to understand there is joy in the morning, but there is another side.

As I sit at my desk and prepare to close this chapter, my mind reflects back to my early morning rising. As I rose up this morning and sat on the side of my bed, the spirit declared, "just as the sun sets and ushers in the night, it will rise again as the bright sun shines. " To the reader, I laid down and had the assurance that I would rise up again with new strength for today. So, it is with the griever every day will be a day of new awakenings. To be awakened is the act of waking from sleep. It is the act or moment of becoming suddenly aware of something. What will you be awakened to? Hope Beyond Your Tears"! You will be graced to know that life will continue with you as a part of it. It will be your life that ushers in hope to hopeless people.

Like Peter and the disciples, as your tears begin to fade away, you will understand that you have been given grace for grief. What is grace? Grace is unmerited divine assistance given to humans for their regeneration. It is virtue coming from God alone. This grace will be the supernatural and will usher you the griever into your next level of living known as "Hope Beyond Your Tears"!

CONCLUSION

Could you hear it? Tick, tock, tick tock, the sound is getting louder. Listen and pay close attention. The clock is ticking; you have no time to waste.

Often times when you hear the phrase, your clock is ticking". It means the time (for something to be done) is passing quickly. It suggests you hurry up. This allusion is to a stopwatch is often used as an admonition to speed something up. As you walk through your process of grief, please remember your time is in the Creators' hands Psalms 31:15

God, the all-sufficient one, creator of all things, has a purpose for each event that has taken place in our lives. Some events are joyful, and others are painful, but He works it together for our good Romans 8:28.

Daily as a griever, I am learning that people are only given to us for a season, and we are to make each moment count. James puts it like this, whereas ye know not what shall be on the morrow, for what is your life? It is even a vapor that appeared for a bit of time and then vanishes away. James 4:14

Matthew Henry puts it like this the frailty, shortness, and uncertainty of life, ought to check the vanity and presumptuous confidence of all projects for futurity. We can fix the hour and minute of the suns rising and setting tomorrow, but we cannot fix the particular time of vapor being scattered.

So short, unreal, and fading is human life. All the prosperity or enjoyment that it attends. However, bliss or woe forever must be according to our conduct during this fleeting moment. We are always to depend on the will of God. Our times are not in our own hands but at the disposal of God. As we recognize our moments, I believe that our load of sorrow and grief will become one of laughter and hope.

Indeed, the road the griever walks on starts out narrow, but on the journey, they will one day look up and see that they are not walking on the path alone. With their heads held high, they will begin to decree and declare there is hope beyond my tears.

As I close, I could see my brother standing before me singing one of his favorite songs written by Earth, Wind, and Fire; "Keep Your Head to The Sky."

The song says, keep my head to the sky for the clouds to tell me why. As I grow and strengthened, Master kept me as I repent, and he said," Keep your head to the sky.

In my prophetic voice, you can now look up, for there is hope beyond your tears. Selah

Prayer of Comfort

Great God Be Big enough to hear us now!

Father, it is with a humble submission that you create a clean heart in us and renew a right spirit within. As we submit to you today, we confess that we are weak, and you are strong.

You declared that if we waited upon you, you would renew our strength and cause us to mount up on wings of eagles. We submit the seat of our emotions into your hands today; so that in exchange, your joy will produce strength for our tomorrow.

We decree and declare that we will be given beauty for ash and the oil of joy for our mourning on this day. We come against the enemy's plot and declare that the spirit of oppression and depression is bound by the neck. We now receive peace for every area of our lives.

On this day, we recognize that your grace is sufficient; therefore, we will enter into your gates with thanksgiving and into Your courts with praise.

Father, you promised to be the good shepherd that would lay us down beside still waters. We decree and declare that we lack nothing, and you, oh Lord, will refresh our soul. You will guide us along the right paths for your namesake. Even though we walk through the darkest valley, we will fear no evil. For indeed, your rod and staff will comfort us. Therefore, make us that tree that is planted by the rivers of living waters.

Father fix our hearts, for you told us to cast all of our cares upon you because you care. I ask that you lift up the bow down head and strengthen the feeble knees and let your river of life flow in me and through me.

Today I will declare that the weak have been made strong, and the poor have been made rich. Father, my heart rejoices in you and you, oh Lord Will I lift up my horn. My mouth will boast over my enemies, for I delight in your deliverance. There is no one holy like the Lord; there is no one besides you: there is no rock like our God. The bows of the warrior are broken, but those who stumble are armed with strength. The barren will barren no more! Lord, you bring death, and you make alive. The foundations of the earth are yours.

Today Father, I declare your kingdom has come, and your will is done, and I shall have hope beyond my tears.

Humbly submitted by the author

Johnnie Mae McCall

THINGS TO REMEMBER

1. Place of Solace

What does a place of solace look like? Remember what the word solace means. It's a place of comfort or consolation of distress or sadness.

Consolation is comfort received by a person after a loss or disappointment

2. The following places are known as places of solace

• God our Father

Is a parental title given to God in many monotheistic religions, particularly patriarchal, Abrahamic ones? In Judaism, God is called Father because he is the creator, life-giver, law-giver, and protector. In traditional Christianity, God is also called Father because of the father-Son relationship revealed by Jesus Christ and the reasons mentioned above.

• Worship Center or a Church

A building that is used for public Christian worship.

A particular Christian organization, typically one with its own clergy, buildings, and distinctive doctrines

- **Word of God**

A manifestation of the mind and will of God; Holy Bible

- **Counseling/Counselor**

The provision of assistance and guidance in resolving personal, social, or psychological problems and difficulties

- **Prayer**

A Solomon request for help or expression of thanks addressed to God or an object of worship.

RESOURCES

You & God- Dedicate a quiet place in your home and carve out a specific time to communion with the creator.

Connect with the following Prayer Lines:

Prayer Meetings

A place where communities gather for the sake of strengthening one another

>Email us, and we will direct you to 2018jmae@gmail.com

- **Grief Ministries**

Specialize and deal with only those that grieve. This ministry will assist the griever in walking out of their grief process.

- **Pastor/Minister (Anyone of the fivefold ministry gifts**

Ephesians 4

When he ascended up on high, he led captivity captive and gave the church gifts for the perfecting and building up of the body. Until we all become that one new man. These are the ministry gifts: Apostle, prophets, evangelists, and some pastors and teachers

- **Family and Friends**

Those you are connected to by bloodline, your extended family, better known as your church community.

- **Various websites**

We list internet sites that will empower you to live; and courage you to go forward.

- **Healing Ministries**

Is a ministry that practices healing arts to facilitate spiritual growth and development in their clients and in their communities

Referral – Elijah Inner Healing School

Urban Mission- Jersey City, NJ (offer the classes)

Visit http://www.bakerpubhlishing.com and look up the book Deliverance and Inner Healing rev (John Loren Sandford and Mark Sandford)

3. Remember You Have Been Given Grace

REFERENCES

- What So Amazing about Grace - Phillip Yancey
- The Awakening: Believing in Grace Is One Thing. Living It Is Another -Charles R. Swindoll
- In The Grip Of Grace – Max Lucado
- Lord, I Need Grace To Make It Today- Devotional Kay Arthur
- A Book of Grace-Filled Days – Margaret
- WWW.Tentmaker.org/quotes/grace_quots.htnl
- BibleGateway
- New King James Version
- New Living Translation of Bible 2007
- Matthew Henry Concise Commentary
- Wikipedia Free Encyclopedia

- Merriam-Webster Dictionary
- WWW.Tentmaker.org/quotes/grace_quots.html.
- Quotes 101 www.goodreads,com/quotes/tag/darkness
- Parallel Translation of Bible
- Cruentus lyric
- Google search - what is true worshiper?
- Bishop George Searight – Dwelling Place
- RBC.org
- Our Daily Bread
- www.truthmagazine.com
- Think Exist.com Quotes

Wikipedia Dictionary

http://www.the freedictionary.com

NIKJV Bible

KJV Bible

Bibliography
Evangelist Johnnie Mae McCall

Johnnie Mae McCall is an anointed multi-gifted inspirational, motivational, and seminar speaker. She is the Founder and CEO of the Embrace of the Father Ministry.

This ministry provides hope for the hopeless and embraces and empowers many to walk in a purpose-driven life. She is the author of the Embrace of the Father, and Healing is the Children's Bread. She is a member of the New Jersey Strategic Network of Intercessors. For 13 years, she has sponsored the Adopt the Senior Program for the senior citizens in her community.

Johnnie Mae is submitted under the Leadership of Apostle Cierra Lashaun Jones. She is a member of The United Kingdom Global Impact Alliance Prophetic Conservatory. Under this leadership, she attends the School of the Prophets. UK Conservatory Alliance and sit under the Mantel and Mentorship Program.

Johnnie Mae has obtained her Bachelor/Associates' degree, and Master's degree in Theology from the United Christian Bible School accredited through the Jameson Christian College. Dr. James P. Williams serves as Dean. She has worked for over 36 years as a Business Administrator for Goldman Sachs & Co. Johnnie is very dedicated to hospital, prison, and street ministry. She is one of 6 siblings. You will always hear her declare, "We must become the literal embrace from above.

Just as the Father Embraced us, we should embrace others."

Contact Me

You can reach me on my social media outlets at:
Facebook @ johnnie.mccall

Email me @ 2018jmae@gmail.com

www.ingramcontent.com/pod-product-compliance
Lightning Source LLC
Chambersburg PA
CBHW070552170426
43201CB00012B/1816